Editorial Director: Carrie Bolin
Editor: Kim Schworm Acosta
Art Director: Chris Opheim
Designers: Chris Grine & Jack Pullen
Production Design: Dan Horton
Written by: Chris Brethwaite
Contributing Writers: Linda Barnes, Suzanne Berry, Andrew Blackburn, Ellen Brenneman,
Meg Burik, Bev Carlson, Renee Daniels, Stacey Donovan, Andre du Broc, Jennifer Fujita,
Bill Gray, Suzanne Heins, Diana Manning, Tom Shay-Zapien, Dan Taylor, Drew Wagner,
Molly Wigand, John Wurth

ISBN: 978-1-59530-741-5
BOK2169

Made in China
DEC15

Table of Contents

(Can't Do Much Else With 'Em)

They say it's a man's world. And taking a quick look around the old planet, that would certainly explain a lot. Yes, what can you say about men that doesn't immediately conjure up a string of four-letter words— probably not a whole lot. But a good belly laugh? Just read the following and judge for yourself.

(and Eat) to That!

I'm something of a foodie in that I'm picky about what I eat. If it isn't high in fat and calories you're not going to find it on my plate. Hey, if the man upstairs wanted me to eat healthy, he'd have given me a cottontail and floppy ears. And don't get me started on drinking. On second thought, please get me started on drinking.

No Pain,

No Problem

I've been in shape for quite a few years. Unfortunately, it's the shape of an old lady. My feeling is that if I have enough strength to wrestle the cardboard lid off a half-gallon tub of triple fudge ripple, I've got nothing to worry about. Well, except maybe clogged arteries and passing out after climbing up a stair or two, says my doctor. But why should I believe *him?* I'm still trying to figure out who can cure my enlarged medical bill.

Time to Complain

I'll be honest, I don't mind going to work. It's the eight hours I spend there that kills me. Actually, work gives you a sense of purpose in life. It also gives you headaches, ulcers, and enough stress to pop diamonds out your you-know-what, but I digress. So grab a five-dollar latte, kick off your shoes, and pretend the boss just called in to say he'll be late.

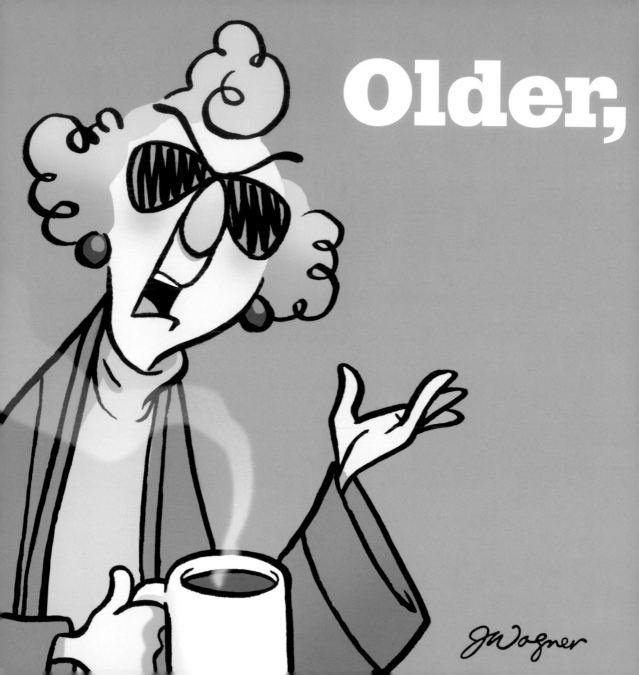

but Whinier

Time marches on, and judging by how I feel, it's doubled back a time or two. And though there's nothing we can do about all the things that droop, sag, ache, and wrinkle, we can still shake our fist at Mother Nature— and hopefully without seeing too much flabby arm jiggle. Now, what was I saying?

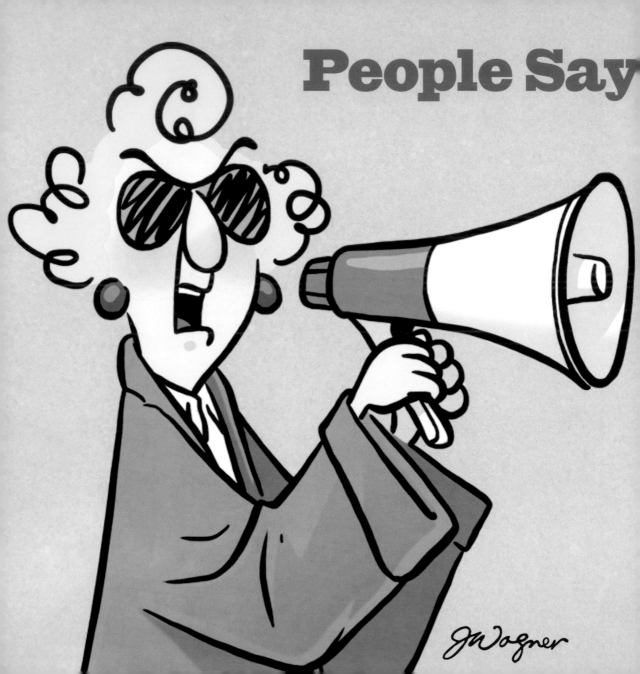

I wish it weren't the case, but some people are difficult and hard to get along with. In fact, there's a name for these people: friends and relatives. And let's not forget everybody else we interact with on a daily basis who makes us want to commit road rage on the highway of life. In any event, we can't blame all of life's aggravations, frustrations, and disappointments on others, but we can certainly try.

and No Sense

Some people say it takes money to make money. I believe 'em—those color copiers don't come cheap. But seriously, financial security is one of the most important things in life. It's right up there with flushable wipes and boneless chicken wings. Fortunately, I'm one of the lucky ones. I have enough money to last the rest of my life. Or a week from Tuesday, whichever comes first.

Word About Technology...
#@%&!

Being old, old, old school, I'm willing to admit I'm somewhat technologically challenged. I miss the old days when "text" referred to words in a book and the only wall I posted stuff to was in my office. But I guess there's no turning back the clock, especially nowadays, when you have to download the freakin' instructions off the Internet just to learn how to do it.

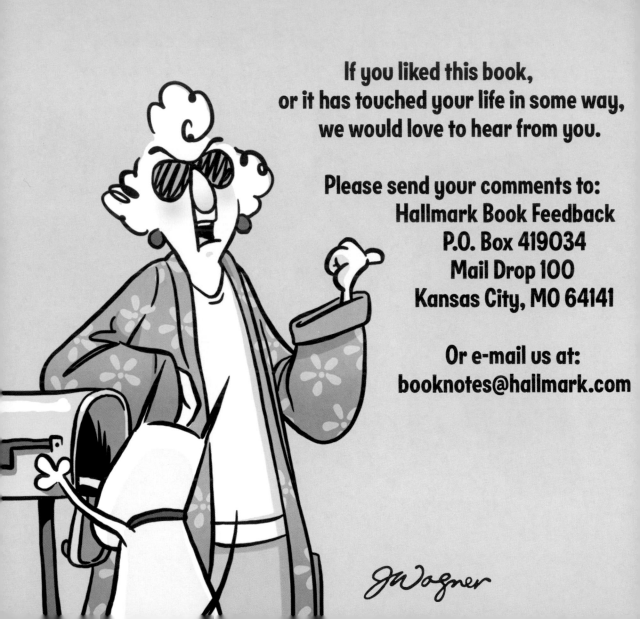